BRITAIN IN OLD PHOTOGRAPHS

FULHAM

CHRISTINE BAYLISS &

JANE KIMBER

LONDON BOROUGH OF HAMMERSMITH AND FULHAM

SUTTON PUBLISHING LIMITED

Sutton Publishing Limited
Phoenix Mill · Thrupp · Stroud
Gloucestershire · GL5 2BU

First published 1996

Cover photographs: *front*: Fulham from the
Putney foreshore, *c.* 1882; *back*: Fulham Bridge
and the toll-house in 1868.

British Library Cataloguing in Publication Data
A catalogue record for this book is available from the
British Library.

ISBN 0-7509-1231-6

Typeset in 10/12 Perpetua.
Typesetting and origination by
Sutton Publishing Limited.
Printed in Great Britain by
Ebenezer Baylis, Worcester.

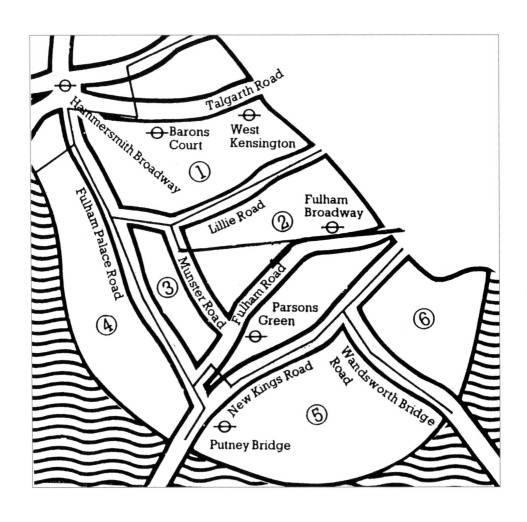

CONTENTS

A workman tending the coal-fired muffle kiln at the northern end of the Fulham Pottery site, *c.* 1952. The kiln was used for firing a range of decorative earthenware that was popular from the 1930s to the 1950s. The origins of the Pottery in New Kings Road, which was founded by John Dwight, are believed to date back to 1672. The Pottery passed through various hands and in 1974/75, following a public enquiry, most of the buildings were demolished. A restored bottle kiln alone remains to mark the site.

INTRODUCTION

Fulham is an area of London which has changed its character several times. Until the nineteenth century three factors defined its development: the proximity of the River Thames, the richness of the soil and its convenient distance from the city. Over the last 150 years it has evolved from a suburb of the encroaching metropolis into an increasingly fashionable part of London.

There was settlement along the Thames at Fulham in Neolithic times, and during the Roman period in the third and fourth centuries AD. The name Fulham probably derives from the name of an Anglo-Saxon man, 'Fulla', combined with 'hamm', which means low-lying land in the bend of a river. In 704 the Manor of Fulham was granted to Waldhere, Bishop of London, thus beginning a long connection with the Bishops of London which only ended in 1973. Fulham Palace, the oldest surviving part of which dates from 1480, was long the country residence of the bishops. The parish of Fulham included Hammersmith until 1834.

Riverside industries included fishing, basket-making, oast houses and lime kilns. The river could only be crossed by ferry until 1729, when a timber toll-bridge was built. It was intended to last fifty years, but in the end did duty until 1886, when the present Putney Bridge was built to the designs of Sir Joseph Bazalgette. Further north, the soil was ideal for orchards and market gardens and from the seventeenth century onwards Fulham provided fruit and vegetables for the London market. It was also an important area for nursery gardens, and among those who introduced new trees and plants to this country were two of the Bishops of London: Edmund Grindal, who imported the tamarisk tree to England, and Henry Compton, who grew the first *magnolia virginiana* in Europe at Fulham.

Parsons Green, North End and Fulham Town, which had as its focal point the parish church of All Saints, were well-established villages by the eighteenth century, while Walham Green, where the stocks, whipping post and parish pound were sited, developed a more working-class character. Most properties in Fulham were cottages, but a number of houses were erected by wealthy families, most of which have now vanished: Brandenburgh House, built on the river at Crabtree by the slave trader and Royalist Sir Nicholas Crisp and later home to the ill-fated Caroline of Brunswick, wife of George IV (his morganatic wife, Mrs Fitzherbert, lived at East End House, Parsons Green); Craven Cottage, where Bulwer-Lytton entertained the future Napoleon III; The Grange in North End, home of the novelist Samuel Richardson and later the artist Sir Edward Burne-Jones; Peterborough House, visited by John Evelyn and Voltaire, and other houses with charming names; Rosebank at Crabtree, Willow Bank near Fulham Bridge, Broom House, Ranelagh House and Mulgrave House in Hurlingham. Some of the big houses later became schools or asylums before being pulled down and their grounds eventually built over.

Arable farming and market gardening were the chief local occupations until the mid-nineteenth century. Among those who found employment were the Irish fleeing from the potato famine in the 1840s. Other main industries, apart from some riverside activities, were Fulham Pottery, founded by John Dwight in 1672 in New Kings Road, and the Swan Brewery at Walham Green. In the nineteenth century, somewhat later than in other London suburbs, improvements in communications and the outward spread of the metropolis encouraged the growth of industries and the development of new streets of houses by speculative builders. In Fulham it was the horse bus services rather than railways which attracted new residents at first, although the Metropolitan District Line did extend southwards to Putney Bridge in 1880. Sands End, originally a quiet backwater, had already begun to change in the early nineteenth century when the Imperial Gas, Light and Coke Company built a gas works there, and the building of Wandsworth Bridge in 1873 further stimulated development. Fulham Power Station, run by the local authority, was built in Sands End at the turn of the twentieth century, and was served by the Borough's own fleet of colliers. Industrial enterprises in that locality included Kops Brewery, MacFarlane Lang's biscuit factory, William De Morgan's tile manufactory and various wharves and heavy industrial enterprises. Manbré and Garton, sugar manufacturers, were sited further north on the riverfront at Crabtree. Other important industries in Fulham were oil company depots, omnibus and railway works and laundries. By 1916 there were over 200 factories in Fulham.

Houses were needed for the workers in these industries and for the more well-to-do people, for whom Fulham was an attractive dormitory suburb. The population of Fulham, according to the census returns, rose from 9,319 in 1841, to 15,539 in 1861, 42,895 in 1881 and 91,640 in 1891. Speculative builders such as Jimmy Nichols and the partners Gibbs and Flew were active in the last quarter of the nineteenth century. The northern part of Fulham, Barons Court and North End for example, was respectable with its developments of mansion blocks and big terraced houses, while the southern part was less exclusive. Meanwhile new facilities, both municipal and private, were needed by the expanding population. Fulham Workhouse was built in 1850, its infirmary later evolving into Fulham Hospital, which was rebuilt in 1973 as part of the new Charing Cross Hospital. Fulham Cemetery (1865), the first Fulham Library (1887), Fulham Town Hall (1890), Bishops Park (1893) and Fulham Baths and Wash-houses (1902) were provided by the Vestry and its successor the Metropolitan Borough of Fulham. The Grand Theatre opened in 1897 and the Granville Theatre, designed by Frank Matcham, in 1898. Fulham Football Club took its name in 1889 and Chelsea Football Club, just inside Fulham at Stamford Bridge, was founded in 1905. For those who preferred to be players rather than spectators, Queen's Club and Hurlingham Club provided sporting opportunities for the better-off.

After the First World War, unemployment and overcrowding became a problem. The majority of houses in the Metropolitan Borough of Fulham were in multi-user occupation and there were long-established slums in certain areas, such as Fulham Fields, where labourers had pulled cabbages in the nineteenth century, and in the streets around Fulham Broadway. After the Second World War, during which Fulham suffered its share of bomb damage, the population declined from its 1921 peak of 157,938 and slum clearance and municipal housing developments gathered pace. In the late 1960s a process of gentrification started on the borders with Chelsea which has now spread to much of the area. Only the northern part of Fulham, where the late-nineteenth century terraced houses have been divided into small flats and bedsits, has resisted this process. Office blocks have replaced factories, many industries have gone from the river frontage and Chelsea Creek has been reborn as the upmarket Chelsea Harbour. The tide of change continues in Fulham.

All the pictures in this book have been selected from the collection of more than 60,000 photographs held at Hammersmith and Fulham Archives and Local History Centre. Thanks are offered in particular to the following for granting permission to reproduce certain photographs in the book, with apologies for any omissions: Head Teacher and Governors of All Saints C of E Primary School, Mr R. Allison, Mrs T. Bradley, Mrs J. Clough, Mr E. Forge, Mr A.T. Gould, Mrs G. V. Grindley, Mr B. Kingwell, Mr and Mrs J. Martin, Mr A.W. Parsons, Mr and Mrs B. Record, Renault UK Ltd, Mrs M. Russell, Mr A.P. Smith, Mr G. Stone, Mr D. Turner. The authors would also like to thank the staff of Hammersmith and Fulham Reference Libraries for their assistance.

MARGRAVINE &
WEST KENSINGTON

The Queen's Club Dairy at 92 May Street, probably in the 1930s. Jones Bros, who are recorded in local street directories at this address between 1923 and 1938, also sold eggs, butter and honey.

Mornington Lodge in North End Road, *c.* 1897. This property, in the centre of the photo, was built in about 1834. Its occupants included William Henry Gibbs who purchased it in 1878 and subsequently enlarged it. Both independently and in partnership with Mr J.P. Flew, he built large parts of Fulham. The house was demolished in 1929 and Pelham House, a block of flats, now occupies the site.

A traffic-free view of the Three Kings Hotel and West Kensington Station in North End Road, 1907. The attractive houses to the left of the hotel are no longer there, having been demolished to make way for the Cromwell Road extension. The hotel had been rebuilt in 1902 to replace an older building dating back to the mid-1700s.

'Monday morning at the Police Court' is the caption to this photograph taken in 1895 and published in Feret's *Fulham Old and New* in 1900. Judging by the crowds outside the court, which was situated in Vernon Street, it looks as though Fulham had just experienced a rather lawless weekend. The Court, built in the late 1850s, replaced an earlier building in Brook Green. In turn this building was superseded in 1915, and now a new West London Magistrates Court has recently been erected in Talgarth Road. While the court pictured above was being rebuilt, a temporary court was erected on the site of the old cells and offices. The solicitors' table had originally 'done duty' in the House of Lords.

A view of Adeney Road from Fulham Cross probably taken in about 1907. Adeney Road with its small-scale housing and neighbourly atmosphere was demolished in the mid-1970s, along with houses in several surrounding streets, to make way for the Bayonne Road Estate, later known as the Brecon Estate, which was built by the Greater London Council.

A view of Greyhound Road taken from Fulham Palace Road, *c.* 1905. The billboards outside the newsagents shop carry headlines that seem to refer to the Russo-Japanese War, 1904/5. President Theodore Roosevelt, whose name also appears, received the Nobel Peace Prize in 1906 for brokering the peace between the two warring countries.

Despite the poor condition of this photograph, the elaborate decorations erected by the Langston family to celebrate the Diamond Jubilee of Queen Victoria in June 1897 can be clearly seen. David John Langston and William Langston were locksmiths, gas and hot water fitters and sanitary engineers and can be seen standing in the archway of their premises at 155 (later renumbered 249) North End Road, close to the Seven Stars public house. There was much competition between local shopkeepers and publicans to see who could produce the best decorations, which included fairy lights, Japanese and Chinese lanterns, flags, drapes and portraits of the Queen and her family. The *Fulham Chronicle* of 25 June 1897 reported that: 'Down into aristocratic Barons Court, back into labouring Munster and Margravine, along into Socialist Sands End, there was not a street or a road that did not contain some little sign of illumination in honour of the record reign.'

St Katharine's Convent, Normand House, *c.* 1910, where the St Katharine's Sisterhood looked after thirty girls, who came straight from prison when their sentences ended. After two years training in house, needle and laundry work they were provided with outfits and jobs. The convent and surrounding properties were destroyed during the last war; Normand Park and the Fulham Pools now occupy their sites.

Elderly ladies enjoying the sunshine in the garden of the Fulham Union Workhouse, *c.* 1905. In 1899 new wards that could accommodate over eighty people were opened at the Workhouse, intended for the 'aged and deserving poor'. In addition, the garden immediately in front of the new wards was set aside solely for the use of the occupants of these wards.

Guests and onlookers assembling for the opening of the new chapel built for the use of the inmates of Fulham Union Infirmary. Elizabeth Georgiana Palmer, a former borough resident, offered to build the chapel at her own expense. The offer was accepted and Sir Arthur William Blomfield designed the edifice, which was erected on a site facing Fulham Palace Road a little to the left of the Workhouse. A newspaper report of the event mentioned that: 'In front of the Workhouse a bright array of flags denoted that some thing was astir and proved the means of attracting an expectant crowd around the gates.' The Service of Dedication was conducted by the Bishop of London on 24 January 1890.

The dispensary at Fulham Union Infirmary in 1912, with, left to right, Mr Brown, Mr Tideman and Mr Stuckland. When the Infirmary opened in 1884 it had 486 beds with two doctors and thirty-one nurses to look after the patients. A dispenser was appointed in 1887 and paid the princely sum of £65 per annum for working six days a week.

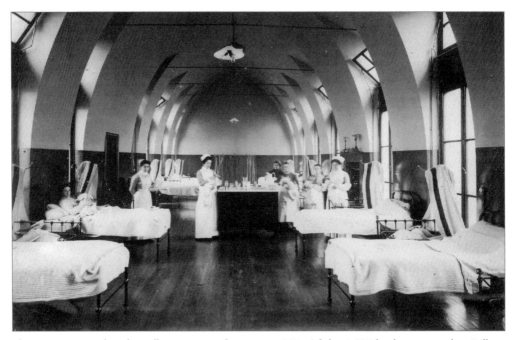

The maternity ward at the Fulham Union Infirmary, *c.* 1907. Of the 4,507 births registered in Fulham during 1907, 125 took place in the Union Infirmary attached to the Workhouse. To save the feelings of these children later on in life, birth certificates gave their place of birth as 103 St Dunstan's Road.

This dramatic photograph shows the demolition of the chimney of the Imperial Tobacco Company's factory in Margravine Road at 2.30 p.m. on 7 April 1936. The site, which had been compulsorily purchased from the company for £17,000 the previous year, was described as being 'a well-built factory with a frontage to Margravine Road of approximately 207 feet and to Lurgan Avenue of approximately 60 feet'. William Morris House, a development planned to accommodate 352 persons at a ratio of 1.5 persons per room, was built in two blocks on the site.

Poppy's Corner. A quiet scene at the junction of Lillie Road with North End Road, *c.* 1901. Poppy's, a mantle manufacturers and ladies' outfitters, occupied 6–13 The Crescent (later renumbered to become 307–311 North End Road and 86 and 86a–d Lillie Road) from about 1900 to 1924.

The display in the right hand window of Lipton's at 46 Greyhound Road in 1926 shows the wide range of teas that Lipton's grew and sold. The manager, Mr Stone, is in the centre of the photograph with Mr Williams standing slightly behind him on his right. In 1938 Mr Williams' wages rose from £2 13s to £2 18s a week.

A view of Castletown Road, taken in the early part of this century. The church on the right, West Kensington Congregational Church, was designed by Messrs James Cubitt and opened on 2 June 1885. It was badly damaged by bombs on 20 February 1944 and the reconstructed church, hall and rooms were opened in October 1955. The building is now the Bharat Vidya Bhavan Indian Cultural Centre.

To photograph this view of the Talgarth Road today, from Glazbury Road, would be to risk life and limb. This picture was probably taken in 1907 shortly after Talgarth Mansions, on both sides of the road, were built. The mansion block on the right was demolished in the late 1950s when the road was widened and the Cromwell Road extended.

Queen's Club Gardens, 1903. The estate, by W.H. Gibbs and Co., was started in 1892 on the site of an old brickfield adjacent to the Queen's Club. The handsome blocks of flats, named after prominent people, contained suites of 3–7 rooms, baths with hot and cold water and were let on rentals of £30 to £100 per annum.

Albert Mews, Field Road, in the early 1930s. These mews, mostly occupied by street traders, lay on two sides of a large common courtyard. Living accommodation was on the first floor while the ground floors were used as stables or for the storage of goods such as vegetables. Mary Macarthur House was subsequently built on the site just before the Second World War.

The construction of Gwendwr Gardens in the early part of 1949. This small triangular site at the junction of Gunterstone Road and Gwendwr Road, formerly the Cedars Lawn Tennis Club, was offered to the Council by the Gunter Estate in 1948. It was given on the understanding that it would be laid out as a memorial pleasure ground for nearby residents and that it would commemorate the extensive damage that the area had suffered through enemy action, particularly on the night of 20 August 1944. Mr Gunter contributed towards the cost of laying out the gardens, which were opened on 23 July 1949.

Lillie Walk, a short narrow street running parallel to Moylan Road and Tilton Street, with numbers 42–2 on the right. Originally known as Church Path, it was renamed Lillie Walk in 1936. This photograph is believed to have been taken in about 1955, shortly before the houses were demolished to make way for St Augustine's RC Primary School.

No. 18 Fane Street, c. 1930. The caption to this photograph, published in the journal of the Fulham Housing Association in 1931, was: 'A Fulham front door. (A horse uses the further door).' In May 1932 the Medical Officer of Health described 18 and 20 Fane Street as being in a 'very dilapidated and insanitary condition', and the premises were vacated soon after.

The garden of The Grange, 40 North End Crescent, formerly 111 North End Road, possibly taken in the 1930s. The Grange was one of a pair of houses built in 1714 by John Smith, Master of the Armourers' Company in 1703. It is mainly known for its two famous residents: Samuel Richardson, the novelist, and Sir Edward Burne-Jones, the artist. Richardson used it as a country house for weekend visits and wrote *Clarissa Harlowe*, *Pamela* and *Sir Charles Grandison* during his tenancy between 1738 and 1754. Edward Burne-Jones, who was created a Baronet in 1894, lived and worked at The Grange from 1867 until his death in 1898. The designer and socialist William Morris, who lived at Hammersmith, was a regular visitor for Sunday breakfast. Later the house was occupied for some years by the Crowther family who displayed monuments, statues and other architectural stonework there. Some of these pieces can be seen in the photograph. The house became derelict and despite a campaign to save it, was demolished in 1957.

This interestingly shaped building, the Empress State Building off Lillie Road, was built by Walter Lawrence & Son Ltd. to the designs of Stone, Toms & Partners, and opened in 1962. Over 300 feet high, its twenty-seven floors were served by twelve of the most modern passenger lifts and three firemen's passenger or goods lifts. Occupied since completion by the Ministry of Defence, this local landmark takes its name from the Empress Hall which had previously stood on the site. The hall was part of the Earl's Court complex and was built to house part of an exhibition mounted in celebration of Queen Victoria's assumption of the title Empress of India.

WALHAM GREEN &
FULHAM BROADWAY

A view of the Fulham Cross area looking west along Lillie Road, c. 1905. The property on the right, built as the Queen Anne public house but never licensed, became a coffee house. Twynholm Baptist Church, founded in 1891, took over the building for its mission hall in 1893 and continued using the ground floor as a coffee palace. 'It is, in fact, nothing more or less than a poor man's restaurant', commented a local newspaper.

A row of old tenements in Rylston Road, demolished in 1897. Clyde Flats, a large block of artisans' dwellings, were erected on the site in the following year. Local historian C.J. Feret commented that the cottages had been 'long inhabited by some Welsh women whose national costume, as they worked in the market garden grounds, was always a picturesque sight'.

A row of quaint tenements named Pond Place, that ran between Farm Lane and the north end of Jerdan Place, seen here in 1895. The name refers to the old pond that stood on the site of St John's Church, built in 1827/8. The shop on the right of the photograph is displaying a wide range of birdcages and dovecotes.

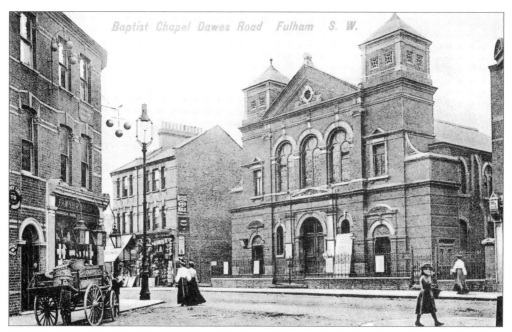

Fulham Baptist Church, Dawes Road, *c.* 1905. Designed by Charles Bell, it opened on 9 May 1889. It cost £3,500 and seated 750 persons, but still needed a further extension in 1906. A pawnbroker's shop, with its traditional sign, can be seen on the left of the photograph.

The reason for this mass attempt to save souls outside Walham Green Wesleyan Chapel in Fulham Road in the mid-1930s is not known. The origins of the church date back to about 1811 when services were held in a small building known as Salem Chapel. It was replaced by an iron chapel until the opening of the permanent church in 1892. When this closed in 1965, the congregation merged with Walham Grove Methodist Church until the new Fulham Broadway Methodist Church opened in 1971 in Fulham Road.

The Revd John Frost with members of the Mothers Union photographed outside St Augustine's Church, Lillie Road, possibly in late 1940. Mr Frost, who was vicar of the church from 1940 to 1948, was inducted on 13 October 1940. Sadly, two days later his church was destroyed by a bomb and services had to be held in the church hall.

A view of North End Road looking north from its junction with Dawes Road, c. 1904. The tall pedimented building on the left housed the Fulham Baths which were opened in 1902. St John's Church, on the right, was designed by Mr Taylor and consecrated on 14 August 1828. Major internal alterations to provide a new parish centre were carried out in 1988/9.

Barbers department store, North End Road, *c.* 1924. Frederick Holgate Barber, later Mayor of Fulham, opened a small draper's shop in 1891. Closing hours then were 9 p.m. on Monday, Tuesday and Wednesday; 2 p.m. on Thursday; 10 p.m. on Friday and 11 p.m. on Saturday. Eventually the business expanded to occupy the entire block between Estcourt Road and Armadale Road; it closed in the 1990s.

A view of Fulham Broadway taken looking towards Fulham Town Hall, *c.* 1911. Timothy Davies Ltd, whose premises are on the right with a flag advertising their latest sale, was opened as a tiny drapers' shop measuring 30 feet by 18 feet at 9 The Broadway in 1885. The business expanded until by 1936, it had a selling area of approximately 30,000 square feet.

Dear's Corn Stores, 269 Lillie Road, in 1937. The exterior of the shop has been decorated to celebrate the Coronation of George VI on 12 May. Dear's had entered their shop in the *Daily Mail*'s 'Coronation Brighter Britain Campaign', which offered prizes of up to £5,000. The *Fulham Chronicle*, reporting on 14 May on the wide variety of decorations in Fulham, said of Lillie Road: 'Apart from a few streamers across the road at the corner of Pellant Road and a few individual displays, Lillie Road was very sober in its decorations.' Dear's shop mainly sold bird, poultry and animal foods, although eggs, margarine, sugar and tinned salmon were also available.

On 7 June 1926 an articulated lorry smashed into 63 Shorrolds Road. The lorry was driven by Mr Charles Bambridge, who swerved to avoid children playing in the road. He came to a stop in the living-room of eighty-year-old Mr J.P. Shipley, who had been sitting reading at the time of the accident. Both men were unhurt.

The funeral cortège of Alfred Augustus Hilyfield Peters, of 20 Caroline Place, which took place on 21 October 1920. A rifleman with the King's Royal Rifle Corps, he died in Winchester on 14 October 1920, aged eighteen. He was buried in Fulham Cemetery after a service conducted by a Roman Catholic priest.

Fulham Congregational Church and the entrance to St John's C of E Primary School in Dawes Road, *c.* 1905. The church, which was founded in 1880, moved to Fulham in January 1887. It was disbanded in 1944 after the building was badly damaged by bombs, and flats now occupy the site. St John's C of E Primary School moved to this site in 1894.

The Butchers' Almshouses in Vanston Place, *c.* 1912. Founded in 1828, the Butchers' Charitable Institution afforded 'relief to decayed and distressed master butchers, master pork butchers, cattle and meat commission salesmen, and hide and skin salesmen, their widows and orphans'. From 1922 the site has been occupied by the Samuel Lewis Trust Dwellings, with 353 'tenements' providing housing for 1,200 to 1,500 people.

North End Road with an unidentified procession passing down it near Barbers store, possibly in 1919. The men towards the front of the procession are carrying the banner of the Fulham Branch of the Discharged Sailors and Soldiers Federation. Behind them is a large contingent of Boy Scouts. On the left is a van fuelled by gas belonging to Messrs Pontings, the High Street Kensington draper's store. Gas was used as a fuel for motor vehicles during the First World War. It was 'carried in great bags upon the roof which swayed and bellied in the wind'.

Walham Yard, a small turning running parallel to North End Road between Eustace Road and Walham Grove, in October 1952. This is one of a series of photographs taken, it is believed, to show the general conditions in Walham Yard, which was used by market traders for the storage of fish, fruit and vegetables.

No. 2, Estcourt Road and 278–260, North End Road, c. 1905. North End Road School, which was opened in 1881, can be seen near the right hand side of the photograph. It was destroyed by bombs in 1944 and part of the Clem Attlee Estate now occupies the site.

The construction of Block K of Clem Attlee Court on 6 November 1956. This photograph was taken looking towards Dimsdale Road and Coomer Road. Block K, later known as Hugh Gaitskell House, has been demolished in recent months. Clem Attlee Court was opened by Earl Attlee on 21 September 1957, in an area that had suffered extensive war damage.

This photograph of Welford Terrace was taken in about 1931. A small street between Hannell Road and Aintree Street, it was demolished when the Aintree Estate, which opened in 1957, was developed. The Medical Officer of Health advised that the houses should be demolished as 'they had sanitary defects which made them unfit for human habitation'.

This aerial view, taken in 1922, shows part of the Western Hospital and below it the War Seal Mansions – now known as Sir Oswald Stoll Mansions – as well as Stamford Bridge, the home of Chelsea Football Club. Founded in 1916 by Sir Oswald Stoll, the theatrical impresario, the War Seal Mansions provided disabled ex-servicemen and their families with inexpensive flats and medical assistance. Funds were raised by the sale of halfpenny 'war seals', similar to those sold today by various charities, which were stuck on envelopes in addition to postage stamps. Western Hospital, which opened as the Fulham Smallpox Hospital in 1877, was enlarged a number of times, but closed in 1979. A modern housing development, Brompton Park, and London Oratory School now occupy the site. Chelsea Football Club, so named because of its proximity to Chelsea and the prior existence of Fulham Football Club, played its first league game at Stamford Bridge on 9 September 1905. The ground has been much altered over the years.

PARSONS GREEN & MUNSTER

This view of Fulham Road in 1867, looking towards the junction with Fulham High Street, is one of the earliest photographs in the Archive and Local History Centre's collection. The barns on the right are part of the market garden grounds cultivated by Robert Matyear.

These two photographs show the Munster Road Depot, *c.* 1905, and one of its prize-winning occupants. The depot, built for Fulham Vestry, opened in mid-1889 and provided stabling for forty-four horses with the appropriate facilities. The horse in the bottom photograph won a medal in the Cart Horse Parade held in Regents Park on 1 June 1903. The Vestry's, and later the Council's horses regularly won prizes at this event. The horses were very hard-working. In a two week period in 1903 trade refuse and dust amounting to 800 loads, weighing 1,312½ tons, was moved by a team of 270 horses. On average each horse moved nearly 5 tons a day.

Fulham Road looking east from the Marist Convent, *c.* 1905. Arundel Mansions, with the Sunlight Laundry below them, were built on the site of Arundel House, demolished in 1898. The Wheatsheaf, further along the road, was rebuilt in 1890. The building opposite is Fulham Fire Station, opened in 1896.

Harwood Road and the Fulham Town Hall extension, probably in late 1905. The extension was built by Mr F.C. Minter of Putney, whose board can be seen on the building, at a cost of about £24,000. It provided suitable offices for each department so that staff could work under '. . . pleasanter and healthier conditions'. The extension was officially opened on 1 November 1905.

Fulham High Street and The Eight Bells public house, 1896. This part of Fulham High Street led down to Fulham Bridge. When Putney Bridge and a new approach road were built, trade fell off at The Eight Bells. The licensee claimed and eventually won compensation of £1,031 plus interest from the Metropolitan Board of Works.

The White Horse at Parsons Green in the mid-1920s. The origins of this pub, which was rebuilt in 1885/6, probably date back to the late eighteenth century. To the right is the Holt Yates Memorial Home & Laundry for the Friendless and Fallen, one of several buildings in the vicinity caring for disadvantaged young people, and later the site of Fulham Maternity Hospital.

Eelbrook Common on a summer day looking towards Musgrave Crescent from New Kings Road, *c.* 1905. Eelbrook Common, an open space of 14 acres long used for recreational purposes, was acquired by the Metropolitan Board of Works in 1881 at a cost of £7,000. It was transferred to the London Borough of Hammersmith in 1971.

The bandstand at Lillie Road Recreation Ground, *c.* 1913. In 1891 the Ecclesiastical Commissioners sold the land to the Vestry of Fulham for £1,250 an acre. The London County Council paid half the purchase costs and contributed to the laying out of the ground which opened to the public in December 1892.

Fulham Town Hall, *c.* 1903. This imposing edifice, designed by Mr George Edwards and completed in 1890 at a total cost of about £40,000, dominates this part of Fulham Road. It was soon too small and additional extensions were built in Harwood Road in 1905, and in Fulham Road adjacent to the existing building in 1934.

Part of the Fulham Wasteland and Lygon Almshouses, Fulham Palace Road, *c.* 1930. The Almshouses, originally in Dawes Road, moved here in 1886. Homes were provided for six single occupants and eight married couples, with a boardroom for meetings and entertainments. In 1906 six more homes were provided for married couples. The almshouses were rebuilt in 1980.

Fairlawn, the home of the Fulham and South Kensington Branch of the YMCA, *c.* 1905. The house, designed by Andrew Moseley, was built in 1858–60. The YMCA, who had to move from Barclay Road, purchased the freehold for £2,200. They altered the building to provide accommodation for boarders, a meeting hall, library and other necessary offices.

Westfield House, Fulham Road, *c.* 1907. The property was purchased by the Library Commissioners in 1887 for the first public library in Fulham. The library opened on 5 November 1887, and a reading room was built at the rear the following year. The old house and reading room were demolished in 1908 and were replaced by Fulham Library, which opened on 21 October 1909.

A view of Fulham Road looking east from its junction with Munster Road, *c.* 1905. Ward and Cash, drapers, occupied the shop with the lamps on the right from about 1903 to 1907. Harold Laski House, Headquarters of Fulham Labour Party, opened in the property on the right-hand corner in 1952.

No. 28 Parsons Green Lane, June 1907. Asaph A. Prentice had his newsagent's and tobacconist's business here from the late 1890s and it was continued by Arthur Edwin Prentice from about 1924 to 1955. The newspaper flysheets date this photograph to the week beginning 14 June, when the *Evening News* was reporting 'An exciting scene in the City – fire engines and a burglar.'

The showrooms of Fulham Borough Council's Electricity Department at 603 Fulham Road in early 1928. Fulham Vestry decided in 1896 to build its own power station in Townmead Road. The initial cost was £200,000 and power was supplied from February 1901. The showroom opened in 1911 and enabled residents to see what equipment and appliances were available. In 1928, when new showrooms were opened at 587–591 Fulham Road, units of electricity for lighting cost 3½d. Cookers could be hired for between 6s and 8s and irons for 6d per quarter.

One of the milk floats belonging to Robert Record's Parade Dairy, 32 New Kings Road, photographed in about 1922, with 199–205 New Kings Road in the background.

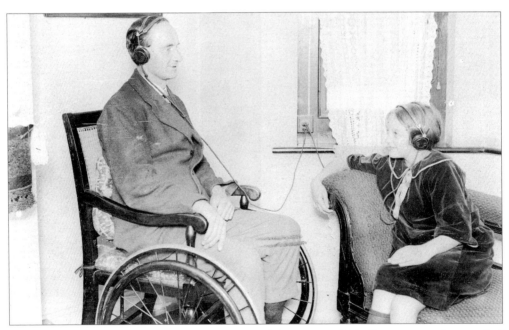

Mr Ripley, a disabled ex-serviceman and resident of the Sir Oswald Stoll Mansions, photographed listening to the wireless on 14 August 1925. The young lady with him is believed to be his grand-daughter. The flats were specially built for the disabled, with facilities such as extra-wide doorways for wheelchairs which made it possible to live comfortably.

Workmen erecting new street lighting outside 173–177 New Kings Road in 1934 attract an inquisitive audience. That summer the Council decided to improve the street lighting in New Kings Road between Britannia Road and Broomhouse Road. The scheme called for the erection of six new columns and the re-spacing of the existing columns so that the distance between them would not exceed 160 feet. The brackets and arc lamps were replaced with diffusing-type lanterns to take 1,000 watt gas-filled lamps. The estimated cost for the work was £560 and it was expected that the extra charge for electricity would be £112 per annum.

A view of Fulham High Street from the offices of International Computers Ltd, taken in 1962. In the last thirty years, traffic density has built up so much that one would only see this number of vehicles in and approaching the High Street early on a Sunday morning.

The 'loo with the view', *c.* 1906. Situated at the junction of Lillie Road and Fulham Palace Road these public conveniences were built in 1905 at a cost of £1,069. They closed in August 1980 and were purchased five years later by architect Paul Brookes, who converted them into an architect's studio with space for about eleven staff.

BISHOPS PARK & CRABTREE

Craven Cottage, c. 1880. This attractive thatched property, built in about 1780, was destroyed by fire on 8 May 1888. It had been built by William, sixth Baron Craven, and contained nineteen rooms sumptuously fitted up in an Egyptian style. The fire was so fierce that a river float had to be deployed from Battersea to quench the flames.

Fulham from the Putney foreshore, *c.* 1882. All Saints Church and Pryor's Bank are in the centre and the aqueduct of the Chelsea Waterworks Company, built in 1855, is on the right. Soon after, the aqueduct was moved temporarily alongside Fulham Bridge, while Putney Bridge, which incorporated a replacement, was built. The barges may have been carrying coal.

A view of the Fulham foreshore showing the buildings between the aqueduct and Fulham Bridge, *c.* 1880. The tower of All Saints Church is to the left, then some oast houses, the coal wharf of Cramer Roberts & Co. and finally Cambridge House.

An aerial view of Manbré & Garton's refinery in Winslow Road, in late 1922. The company's link with Fulham began in the early 1870s when the Manbré Saccharine Company rented part of the site of the Brandenburgh Farm Estate for £400 per annum, '. . . a piece of land with the factories, buildings and works now in course of erection thereon . . . .' The whole factory was ready for production in April 1876. With various name changes the company continued refining sugar and producing sugar products here until the factory closed in the late 1970s. The building was demolished in 1979.

Bishops Walk in 1876. This view shows the tower of All Saints Church before it was rebuilt in 1880/1. The footpath to the right of the moat leads between the rear of Pryor's Bank and John's Place, a group of small cottages demolished in 1882.

Pryor's Bank Pavilion and All Saints Church in 1906. Pryor's Bank Pavilion replaces an older property built in the late 1830s. It was acquired by Fulham Vestry, together with adjacent property, for £4,000 in 1894 and was demolished in 1897. The new pavilion, which sold refreshments, was designed by Charles Botterill and opened at the same time as the extension to Bishops Park in June 1900.

An interior view of the east end of All Saints Church, probably shortly before its closure and demolition in 1880. The old church, dating from the fifteenth century, was described as having a low roof, ugly gallery and small windows. It flooded regularly as there was then no river embankment and the floor level was three feet lower than its replacement. It was closed on 18 April 1880 and demolished, but its tower was retained and forms part of the present structure. The architect for the new church, which was consecrated on 9 July 1881, was Arthur William Blomfield.

Remembrance Day at Fulham War Memorial, 1923. Designed by Alfred Turner, with figures cast in bronze by E.J. Parlanti, the memorial was unveiled on 10 July 1921, a day when 'tropical weather prevailed'. It was located in Fulham Palace Road near the King's Head public house and moved to its present site at the approach to Putney Bridge in 1935.

A view of the paddling pool at Bishops Park, probably in the latter part of 1903. The first part of Bishops Park was opened in 1893 and an extension, which included an ornamental pool and the new and interesting feature of an artificial beach for children, opened in July 1903.

This picturesque building, photographed in 1865, is the Porter's Lodge at Fulham Palace. It was built in about 1820 by William Howley, who was Bishop of London from 1813 to 1828. Fulham Palace was the home of the Bishops of London for several centuries until 1973. It was leased by the London Borough of Hammersmith in 1974, and the gardens and the Museum of Fulham Palace are now open to visitors.

A garden party in the grounds of Fulham Palace, *c.* 1910. Arthur Foley Winnington-Ingram, then Bishop of London, regularly had large groups of visitors at the Palace including many children and their families, bishops attending Lambeth Conferences and members of the Pan-Anglican Congress.

The Bishop's study at Fulham Palace, *c.* 1895. Furnished in a comfortable style, the walls of this room are papered with the 'Indian' design produced by William Morris, in about 1868 to 1870.

The main entrance to Rosebank in 1896 shortly before demolition. The house, which replaced an earlier one that burnt down in 1864, was to the west of the present site of Holyport Road. It was built and presented to General Sir Montague Scott McMurdo, in recognition of his services as Inspector-General of Volunteers. The figures by the door commemorate this link.

FULHAM TOWN & HURLINGHAM

Stokenchurch Street, one of the roads on the Peterborough Estate, c. 1905. In January 1896 Mr J. Nichols, the builder, advertised for sale the 7–11 roomed houses, built in 1894/5, for between £345 and £520.

Fulham Bridge and the toll-house in 1868. Fulham Bridge was opened to foot passengers on 14 November 1729 and to other traffic fifteen days later. Tolls were charged, ranging from ½*d* to 2*s* 6*d* for foot passengers, animals and coaches and horses. The King paid £100 per annum for himself and his household.

The dismantling of Fulham Bridge in 1886, after the construction of Putney Bridge. The old wooden bridge had been about 786 feet long and 24 feet wide with 26 openings or locks along it. Between 1870 and 1872 three central locks were removed and an iron span inserted to provide a better passageway for passing boats.

A view from St Mary's Church, Putney, showing the construction of Putney Bridge in about 1884 – a little upstream from the old one. It was designed by Sir Joseph W. Bazalgette and opened on 29 May 1886. In the centre of the picture are some old oast houses, now the site of a small sheltered-housing development called Swan Court.

'Up the river', c. 1878. This photograph is remarkably similar to a sketch with this title in various editions of *The Mystery of Edwin Drood*, by Charles Dickens. To the left can be seen Fulham Bridge and the toll-house, while the big house on the right was called Willow Bank.

Broom Cottage and Fern Cottage in Broomhouse Road, *c.* 1910. On the left side of the photograph is the junction with Bell's Alley, a cut through to Peterborough Road, and a gateway leading to the Parsons Green Club, a sports club. Sulivan School, which opened in 1951, now occupies the site of these two cottages.

Although the caption on this photograph in Feret's *Fulham Old and New* reads 'Old Houses in Peterborough Place, 1893', it is clear that beer was sold at the middle property. The building on the left-hand edge of the picture is the Grape Brandy Distillery and one of its ventilating turrets can just be seen.

Two views of the same stretch of Broomhouse Lane taken in 1885 and 1961. They both show the Elizabethan Schools which were founded in 1855 by Laurence Sulivan, of Broom House, in memory of his wife Elizabeth. In 1963, after four years of legal dispute between Fulham Borough Council, the Hurlingham Club and Parsons Green Club concerning the cost of making the road up, Broomhouse Lane was declared to be a new street and the Council was able to begin the necessary work. At the turn of the century it was described as having a 'sylvan quietude'. Sixty-three years later 'the passing of one more fragment of old rural Fulham' was reported.

Daisy Lane in 1895. A rural scene with corn growing in the field on the left. Daisy Lane links Peterborough Road and Broomhouse Lane near the junction with the Elizabethan Schools and was made up at the same time as Broomhouse Lane in 1963. The cost of the work done on these two roads was £24,257.

Hurlingham Lodge, 1895. This imposing mansion in Hurlingham Road was built in about 1856 by Mr Andrew Moseley, who named it Edenhurst. In 1946 it became a Red Cross Convalescent Home and later a hostel for men with chronic tuberculosis. It has now reverted to private ownership and has an artist's studio in its grounds.

Peterborough House and its grounds, *c.* 1895. This mansion replaced a much earlier house demolished in 1798, the home of the Mordaunt family; the name derives from the fact that Charles Mordaunt inherited the Earldom of Peterborough in 1697. In later years, before demolition in 1898, it was used as a lunatic asylum. The grounds of the house extended to over twelve acres and contained an ice-well and many fine trees including elm, beech, oak, ash and sycamore. The site is now covered by the Peterborough Estate which was built by Mr James Nichols. He had started building operations some years in advance of the demolition of the house when building land became available.

An aerial view of Sulivan Court taken on 24 November 1955. The view takes in South Park to the north, and the Elizabethan Schools and parts of the Hurlingham Club and Hurlingham Park to the south. Sulivan Court was built on what had been the No. 2 polo ground of the Hurlingham Club. The ground was acquired by Fulham Borough Council after the Second World War, and work started on the 12½ acre site in September 1949, to the designs of Mr J. Pritchard Lovell. The first blocks were opened in November 1950 and the completion ceremony was held on 4 February 1956. The name commemorates the Sulivan family, who were closely associated with the borough for many years.

SANDS END

SS Fulham II, a collier owned by Fulham Borough Council which was used for transporting coal to Fulham Power Station. This photograph was probably taken shortly after it was launched on 23 April 1936.

A view of the shops on the west side of Wandsworth Bridge Road between Studdridge Street and Ryecroft Street, *c.* 1910. In the centre of the photograph a young man with a trolley is delivering a consignment of soda syphons to the off-licence at No. 98. They are carefully packed in a divided wicker basket holding six syphons.

The Old Rose public house in Sands End Lane, 1895. Little remains of Sands End Lane, most of it having been incorporated in the late 1890s into the works of the Gas Light and Coke Company. In return for closing it, the company paid £1,000 to the Fulham District Board of Works and built Imperial Road as a replacement.

South Library in Wandsworth Bridge Road, *c.* 1905. It was built on land purchased in 1893 for £250 from Miss Charlotte Sulivan. Providing a reading room and reference facilities, it opened on 20 January 1896 and cost £2,600. The building was finally completed in 1901, and stood until 1964 when it was replaced by Sands End Library – now closed and relocated.

'The bookies', a scene photographed, it is believed, in the Wandsworth Bridge Road shortly after the turn of the century. Until betting shops were legalized in March 1963 it was illegal to bet on horse races anywhere other than at the race-track. 'Unofficial' bets were often made in the street with a look-out to spot the approach of a policeman.

Edenvale Street, *c.* 1910, looking towards Fulham Borough Council's Refuse Destructor in Townmead Road, which had come into operation in 1900. The long white ramp that can be seen in the centre of the picture led up to the tipping floor where refuse was deposited before being incinerated. When it became inadequate to cope with the increasing demand, a new destructor was opened in 1928.

A rare photograph showing the construction of new houses in Kilkie Street, later numbered 12–2, in 1899/1900. The road is thought to have been named after a village in County Clare, home of the builder John Madigan.

Flooding in Stephendale Road early this century. The reason for the flooding is unknown but the children playing nearby seem to be enjoying the diversion. Stephendale Road takes its name from Stephen Dale Taylor, son of the original landowner.

Celebrating the Silver Jubilee of King George V and Queen Mary in Oakbury Road, 1935. Celebrations included decorations everywhere, street parties, dinners for 1,000 deserving old-age pensioners and tea parties for the children of the unemployed. In one Fulham street a would-be poet chalked a message on the road: 'Please Mr. Landlord don't be offended, but don't call for rent till Jubilee's ended.'

The launching on 7 December 1935 of the first of a fleet of ten colliers commissioned by Fulham Borough Council, which were to supply Fulham Power Station with 2,000 tons of coal a day. The SS *Fulham* was built by the Burntisland Shipbuilding Co. Ltd. and named by the Mayoress, Mrs S. Vanderhook. The length of the vessel was 238 feet and it carried about 2,390 tons, with a crew of sixteen. Her speed and power trials took place in the Firth of Forth and she began her maiden voyage to London on 13 February 1936, arriving five days later having been delayed by fog.

A view of Chelsea Creek, showing railway land around Chelsea Basin and Lots Road Power Station, *c.* 1922. Coal could come by rail or barge to this 19-acre site where it was unloaded and stored for Fulham Gas Works and nearby Fulham Power Station. It is now the site of Chelsea Harbour, an exclusive housing development and marina. Lots Road Power Station produces electricity for London Underground.

Fulham Gas Works, July 1926. No. 4 gas holder is being rebuilt, with No. 5 holder in the background. Fulham Gas Works are among the oldest in the country and were built on a site purchased in 1824 by the Imperial Gas Light and Coke Company.

Demolition work, prior to reconstruction, of Nos 1 and 2 retort houses at Fulham Gas Works in the early 1900s. The neat piles of bricks and other items would seem to indicate that the workmen are salvaging building materials for re-use. A report in the *Fulham Chronicle* in May 1912 states that: 'Over the dock, close to the reconstructed retort houses, is fixed the coal unloading plant . . . all the retort houses now in use are fitted with coke-handling machinery . . . material taken from the barge into the works is never touched by hand . . . .' The first small gasholder to be constructed at Fulham was built between 1827 and 1830 and is now a listed building. The Gas Works were nationalized in the late 1940s.

WAR

Charles Edward Spackman, VC, with the Prince of Wales at a fund-raising event for London's hospitals, 6 October 1922. Spackman, who lived in Moylan Road, was Fulham's second VC. Aged twenty-seven, he won his award for conspicuous bravery at the battle of Cambrai in 1917.

A clothing store for Belgian refugees at Earls Court during the First World War. Accommodation for about 3,000 refugees was provided here, while others were billeted in various locations in the borough. Beds were arranged on the seating tiers of the Empress Hall, and bathing facilities were provided at Fulham Baths. A tablet marking their sojourn, which can be seen at Fulham Town Hall, was presented on 7 May 1919.

A fleet of First World War ambulances. The message on the back of this photograph from Dora O'Conor reads: 'I am driving an Ambulance in the ASC, it is very interesting work. This is a photo of some of the Ambulances.' Dora served with the 369 Company of the Army Service Corps in 1917.

The timber yard of H.N. Barnes at 40 Peterborough Road, before and after bombing on 31 July 1944. The bomb fell at 3.42 a.m. and caused extensive damage to these and surrounding premises. A report in the *Fulham Chronicle* a few days later read: 'Early Monday morning a 'doodle-bug' fell in Southern England near some business premises which caught fire and blazed furiously.' The Fulham Babies' Hospital at 23 Broomhouse Road, which had three patients at the time, had a lucky escape: '. . . A babies' hospital at the rear of the business premises that caught fire was damaged but miraculously the little patients and staff escaped injury'. There was one fatality resulting from this raid.

This church, West Kensington Congregational Church, was one of the many victims of a bombing raid on Fulham on the night of 20/21 February 1944, when over forty incidents were reported. Services were held, until reconstruction work was completed, in nearby St Andrew's Church Hall. One of the other casualties of that night was Teofani's cigarette factory in Pulton Place, which was gutted. The blaze, apparently, accounted for a particularly 'pungent aroma'.

VJ Day celebrations at Lewis Trust Dwellings, Lisgar Terrace, August 1945. Fulham residents celebrated VJ Day with bonfires (three of them in Burnfoot Avenue), dancing and concerts. There was an acute shortage of cigarettes and the pubs ran dry. The *Fulham Chronicle* reported: 'In some cases a piano was brought out to assist the jollifications and radiograms in front gardens also did good service, as did also accordion players.'

Fund-raising events were often held during the Second World War. For Merchant Navy Week, on 22 to 29 May 1943, the Mayors of Richmond and Fulham competed to see which borough could raise the most money. Richmond won – they raised £3,656 to Fulham's £2,870. The Mayor of Richmond is in this photograph, 'fully robed on a magnificent white charger', as the procession passes through Fulham Broadway.

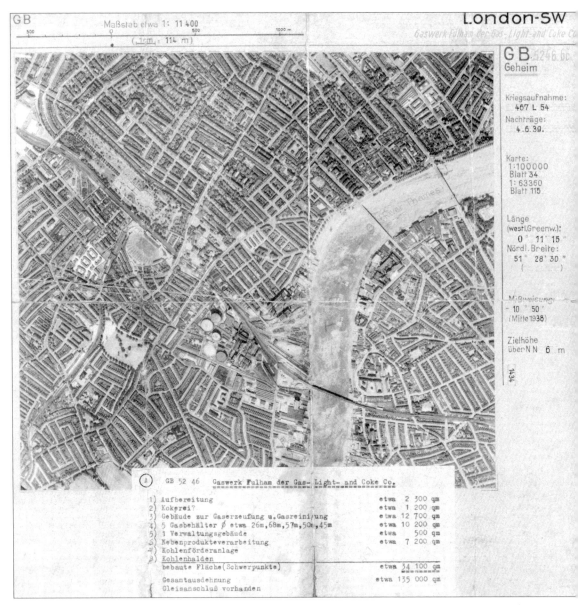

This unusual aerial map showing the location of the different parts of Fulham Gas Works was issued to a German bomber pilot. It was taken from him, after he had escaped from his plane, by a Civil Defence officer. The different parts of the Gas Works are numbered on the map to indicate where the offices, gas holders, coking plant, coal conveyer system and coal stocks were to be found. Additional information was given about the size of the site and its link with the railway system.

SPECIAL OCCASIONS

Preparing 2½ miles of tables for the 14,000 guests at the King's Dinner to the Poor, held in Bishops Park on 5 July 1902 to celebrate Edward VII's Coronation. The menu of roast beef, plum pudding, cheese, chocolate, ale and temperance cordials was served by 2,000 voluntary helpers.

Initial preparation, at Munster Road Depot, of the 4½ tons of new potatoes due to be eaten at the King's Dinner to the Poor. The potatoes were taken to Kops Brewery where they were boiled in huge casks before being packed, sealed and delivered hot to Bishops Park.

Crowds awaiting the arrival of the Prince and Princess of Wales for the King's Dinner to the Poor, 5 July 1902. Two triumphal arches were erected to welcome them, in Bishops Park and at the foot of Putney Bridge. After the dinner, various entertainments and a firework display followed. The celebrations were held even though the King's Coronation had to be postponed because of his illness.

Alexandra Day collectors near Barons Court, June 1918. From left to right: Mrs Stevens, Mrs Whiteley, Mrs Walker, Mrs Perks, Mrs Hammond, Miss Stuart, Miss Danelli and Miss Broom. Alexandra Day is named after Queen Alexandra, consort of King Edward VII, who was noted for her charitable work. The first collection in aid of hospitals was made in 1912.

The Jubilee Drive of King George V and Queen Mary passing along Harwood Road, by the Market Hall, 8 June 1935. Traffic was cleared from the road in advance of the procession with the result that buses took unaccustomed routes, and a bride in her wedding car was seen waving to the crowds. John Wilmot, MP attended at least fifteen children's tea parties that day.

Prince Henry, later HRH The Duke of Gloucester, seen putting a buttercup purchased outside Fulham Town Hall into his buttonhole, 7 May 1924. Buttercup Day was held in aid of the Royal National Orthopaedic Hospital for the Cure of Crippled Children and Adults, of which Prince Henry was president. He arrived at Fulham Town Hall at 2.15 p.m. for a twenty minute visit. The event had been organized by Miss Winifred Broom, daughter of local photographer Mrs Christina Broom. The gentleman in the silk top hat is Sir Kenyon Vaughan-Morgan, MP for Fulham East, 1922–1933, and the lady on the right is the Mayoress, Mrs Waldron.

Celebrations for the Coronation of George VI in Heckfield Place (top) and Orbain Road (bottom), May 1937. The *Fulham Chronicle* reported that: 'The Avenues, with the redevelopment scheme overhanging them have dressed up possibly for the last time. The inhabitants have made a splendid job of it.' Heckfield Place, part of The Avenues, 'has been simply but effectively decorated with red, white and blue garlands of one design strung from house to house practically the length of the place'. Orbain Road was described as being 'literally a blaze of colour. The sky is almost hidden from view by streamers, flags, garlands etc. across the width of the road . . . over the porchway of every house there is a golden crown surmounted with flags.'

Gwyneth Phillips (now better known as Gwyneth Dunwoody) presenting a bouquet to the Mayoress at the Hurlingham Fête, 12 May 1937. The Coronation celebrations there were marred by incessant rain. The most exciting event was a donkey race between the Mayor, Alderman C. Lancaster and Councillor Morgan Phillips, which resulted in a dead heat. Morgan Phillips, who later became General Secretary of the Labour Party, is to the right of the Mayoress.

The visit of Queen Mary to the War Seal Mansions, later Sir Oswald Stoll Mansions, on 5 June 1919. The Queen and Princess Mary were received by Sir Oswald and Lady Stoll and they spent about an hour inspecting the building and chatting to tenants.

The mayor-making ceremony in the Council Chamber at Fulham Town Hall on 9 November 1942, when Councillor Percival James Barton was elected as Mayor from 1942/3. As he was unmarried, his sister Winifred acted as Mayoress during his term of office. The portraits in the Chamber are of King George V (centre) and past mayors.

The official opening of Burne-Jones House, 7 September 1940. The Chairman of the Housing Committee, Percival Barton, can be seen opening the door of No. 62 while the Mayor, Councillor J.A. da Palma looks on. The flats are named after the artist Sir Edward Burne-Jones whose home, The Grange, adjoined the site.

A road race organized by the Western Exits of London Society on 20 November 1926 to demonstrate the need for more roads out of the western side of London. The famous runner Mr T.E. Hammond, of the London Stock Exchange, followed the proposed route between the West Ken Cinema and Chiswick Church and beat the motorist, Councillor Sir Kenyon Vaughan-Morgan, by several minutes. The motorist used the only route available to him, while the runner was able to cross the river by boat and run across private land. The significance of the swastika on the runner's vest is not known; it may have been a club badge or a good luck symbol.

EDUCATION

Children from Infants Class II with their teacher in the playground at Townmead Road School, c. 1910.
The school first opened in a temporary iron building in 1900; the permanent structure opened on 27 March
1905. It closed in 1935, was damaged during the Second World War, and subsequently became the Chelsea
Central Secondary School.

Pupils from All Saints Primary School in the late 1890s, displaying some of the scientific apparatus they used in their lessons. The school was founded in the sixteenth or early seventeenth century in a room over the church porch. Later it occupied buildings in Church Street, now New Kings Road, and moved to its present site in Fulham High Street in 1862.

Children from a local elementary school on a class visit to the Children's Library at Fulham Library in 1923 to use a pre-selected range of books, magazines and encyclopedias for their studies. Lists of subjects to be studied by each child were sent in advance and library staff searched for the material they needed.

Empire Day at Peterborough Road School, 24 May 1909. The Peterborough School Magazine commented on the 1908 day as 'a present time innovation . . . we should learn to regard our flag, the "Union Jack", as the flag of freedom'. The school opened on 26 August 1901. Judging by the number of violinists at the front, they must have had a flourishing school orchestra.

A tidy, well-behaved class at Lillie Road School, c. 1926, with a boy and girl sharing each desk. Now called Sir John Lillie School, it opened in 1893 and was enlarged the following year to accommodate 1,568 children. It is named after Sir John Scott Lillie (1790–1868), who built Lillie Road through the grounds of his house at North End in the late 1820s.

Children from Langford Road School evacuated to Cambridge in September 1939. Their headmistress Miss G. Hobbs is on the right, behind the girl with the triangle. Evacuation of Fulham school children to safe locations began early and they went to Guildford, Midhurst, Windsor and other locations. Langford Road School was used as a mortuary during the war.

Teaching staff of Fulham County Secondary School in 1926. The school was one of the first four secondary schools for girls started by the London County Council. When it opened in 1905 in Finlay Street, 120 girls instead of the expected 60 turned up and found a severe shortage of desks, books and other school paraphernalia. The school moved to Fulham Cross in 1908.

St John's School, *c.* 1894. This school opened in 1836 and was extended in 1846. It was built on an island site in the middle of what was later to become Fulham Broadway. In 1894 the school moved to its present location in Dawes Road and the vacated site was subsequently occupied by the Granville Theatre and offices.

The Marist Convent, Fulham Road, *c.* 1910. Although the Convent School opened on 4 November 1895, the Marist Sisters had already been teaching in Fulham for several years at nearby 24 Bishops Road. The sisters purchased Percy Villa and St Peter's Lodge which were adapted for their purposes. Extensions were added in 1924, 1950 and 1956, but the school closed recently.

Munster Road School. A group photograph of the children from the Boys' School in the playground, c. 1902/3. Munster Road School, which accommodated 1,200 children, opened on 26 June 1893. The building cost £18,850 to erect and the land an additional £3,805.

The Elizabethan Schools in Broomhouse Lane, c. 1895. The building consisted of two almshouses, a girls' school, a boys' school and staff accommodation. They were designed by Horace Francis and opened in 1855. The schools were purchased by the London County Council and tubercular children were taught there from 1921 to 1959. Since 1970 the premises have been used as a youth club.

SECTION TEN

TRANSPORT

A taxicab owned by Messrs Clark and Billings. As Andrew Clark and Thomas William Charles Billing are rated for a house, yard and stable at 2 Star Road from 23 December 1913, this photograph may have been taken shortly afterward.

A view taken from Putney foreshore, *c.* 1883. Behind the Thames barges one can see that construction work on the new Putney Bridge has begun. Cranes are located at each end of the bridge and, on the Fulham side, oast houses where beer was brewed are clearly visible.

Fulham Ferry, *c.* 1870. After the opening of Fulham Bridge in 1729 watermen still continued to ply their trade in direct competition with the tolls charged for crossing the bridge. The waterman in the photograph is probably 'Honest' John Phelps who until shortly before his death in 1890, aged eighty-five, was always ready to ferry people across the river.

A view from Putney Bridge overlooking Swan Wharf and Putney and Hurlingham Station (now Putney Bridge Station), 1904. The Metropolitan District Railway line was extended from West Brompton to Putney in March 1880 and the trellis girder bridge was built when the line was extended to Wimbledon in June 1889. Swan Wharf was purchased by Fulham Borough Council for £12,000 in 1900. Refuse was discharged into the waiting barges through the large wooden chutes that can be seen in the photograph.

A tank engine named *Fulham* being watered, pre-1902. One of the Stroudley 'Terrier' class of engines owned by the London Brighton and South Coast Railway, it was built in June 1877 and withdrawn from service in April 1951 after covering 1,252,822 miles.

Walham Green Station, *c.* 1911. The station opened on 1 March 1880 with the extension of the Metropolitan District Railway from West Brompton to Putney. The frontage of the station was rebuilt in 1910 to the designs of H.W. Ford. After representations from Fulham Chamber of Commerce, it was renamed Fulham Broadway in March 1952.

Chelsea and Fulham Station, on the West London Extension Railway, *c.* 1906. The high proportion of women and children waiting on the platform for their train indicates that this could be a Sunday School outing, perhaps to Brighton which was easily reached from this station. The station has since been demolished.

Horse buses outside The Greyhound public house, Fulham Palace Road, *c.* 1905. The layby off the main road in which two horse buses are standing is still there today. On the left is Fulham Palace Road School (later Melcombe School), which opened in 1902 after moving from temporary premises.

Horse buses crossing Putney Bridge, *c.* 1897. Putney Bridge used to be much narrower than it is now. It was widened between 1931 and 1933 by Messrs Dorman Long and Co., who extended the width of the carriageway from 25 feet to 51 feet, 'without inconvenience to traffic using the bridge'. There was some delay to river traffic passing under the bridge, however.

A tram in Fulham High Street, *c.* 1912. Trams came to Fulham on 23 January 1909, when an electrified route was extended from Hammersmith to Putney Bridge, which entailed the widening of the High Street. Trams were never introduced into central Fulham as the streets around Walham Green were too narrow.

Striking busmen assemble at Walham Green, 6 June 1891. The strike, held on a Sunday, was ostensibly for shorter hours but in reality was linked to the introduction of a ticketing system the previous week, which enabled the companies to keep better control over the revenues collected.

Horse-drawn ambulances at Western Hospital in Seagrave Road, *c.* 1905. Fulham Smallpox Hospital, which opened in 1877 and was extended several times, accepted its last smallpox patients in 1885. It was renamed Western Hospital in 1883 and continued to be used as an isolation hospital for many years. The hospital closed in 1979 and the site is now occupied by Brompton Park, a modern housing development, and part of the London Oratory School.

A charabanc outing to Brighton for the employees of Messrs. Teofani & Co., *c.* 1923. Teofani's were based in Pulton Place, off Fulham Road, and manufactured a range of Turkish cigarettes.

Inside the Seagrave Road workshops of Renault Ltd., 1924. Renault had premises here from 1908. Several well-known car manufacturers were also located in the road. A former employee said: 'We were all there – all the best; Renault, Rolls-Royce and Rover, just opposite the fever hospital.' When Renault left Fulham in the mid-1930s their premises were sold to the Rover Car Company.

Driving instructors from the West London School of Motoring standing by their cars in Ellaline Road, 1937. The school was founded by brothers H. & A. Kingwell in 1936, and had the largest fleet of driving instructors in West London at the time. The decorations on the building are in celebration of the Coronation of King George VI and Queen Elizabeth.

WORK

The London General Omnibus Company's coachworks adjoining their yard in Farm Lane, 1910. It was normal practice to dismantle and overhaul all the company's coaches annually and, as can be seen, new wheels were also made here. The colour of the wheels indicated the company to which the coach belonged.

Crabtree Farm in the 1880s. Edward Matyear, the proprietor of the farm for forty years, is the heavily-bearded gentleman on the right. His obituary in 1910 mentioned that ' . . . practically the whole of the produce . . . has been sold locally . . . it was no uncommon occurrence to see fifty or sixty carts waiting at Crabtree Farm to be served'.

Over 350 staff and employees of the Works, Cleansing and other departments under the control of the Borough Engineer, photographed at Munster Road Depot, 1905. The men in this photograph include bricklayers, masons, farriers, painters, gulleymen, scavengers, sewermen, stablemen, night sweepers, dustmen, drivers, woodpaviours and an assortment of general labourers.

A toll-keeper outside the Putney toll-house on Fulham Bridge, 1880. Toll-houses were situated at each end of the bridge, although the one on the Fulham side was a much grander construction. Tolls of varying amounts were levied from the opening of the bridge in 1729 until 26 June 1880 when Fulham, Hammersmith and Wandsworth Bridges were formally declared to be free of tolls by the Prince of Wales. Despite continual heavy rain that day, the fourteen-mile route followed by the Prince between the bridges was densely crowded.

Some of the outdoor staff at Earls Court, *c.* 1900. Edwin A. Smith (General Foreman) is seated third from left. The first exhibition, which opened here on 9 May 1887, was the American Exhibition and included Buffalo Bill's Wild West Exhibition. In 1895 Imre Kiralfy, who was also connected with Olympia and the White City Exhibitions, became involved in the management of Earls Court.

Fulham Borough Council cemetery employees outside Fulham Cemetery, *c.* 1905. Work must have started early as employees took their breakfasts between 8 and 8.30 a.m. and lunches between 1 and 2 p.m. Gardeners temporarily employed in gravedigging were paid the same as gravediggers during the time they were so employed.

Drayton Paper Works, 1956. The origins of this company, which moved into purpose-built premises in Sulivan Road in 1913/14, date back to 1856. The company produced a wide range of papers and printed items including tickets, bags, boxes and wrapping materials. The works were closed and demolished in 1986.

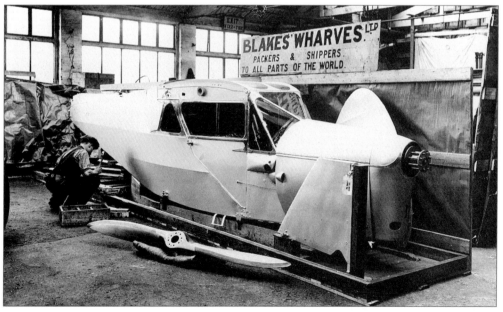

A view of the packing shop at Blakes' Wharves, Stevenage Road, showing a De Havilland Hornet small plane being prepared for transport, c. 1932. Blakes packed and shipped goods to all parts of the world, many of them by water. Munitions were made here during the First World War. The wharves were demolished in the 1970s.

Soldering a window after leading at The Glass House, 1921. The Glass House was founded in 1906 by the firm of Lowndes & Drury and provided specialist facilities for independent designers. Many well-known glass artists, including women, worked in this Grade II listed building in Lettice Street which was designed by C.H.B. Quennell. It closed in 1993.

Mr W. Jones checking the quality of a flower vase at the Fulham Pottery after its removal from a mould, 1952. The vase is from the Fulham Flower Vase range, made from specially blended North Devon clays which were heavily glazed on the inside and had a matt exterior. They cost from 9s to 28s 6d.

Display stand of the Fulham Pottery at the British Industries Fair at White City in 1937. The new range of 'Alber ware', later called Fulham ware, was exhibited for the first time this year. It included vases, mantel vases and wall brackets in both moulded and thrown forms. Designers of this range included Constance Spry, Gerard de Witt and W.J. Marriner. The latter retired from the pottery in 1946 after fifty years service. In his earlier years he had been employed making hot-water bottles. The figure at the corner of the stand was probably part of the 'Christopher Robin' series of garden ornaments, introduced in 1934.

Fulham Wash-houses and Laundry, *c.* 1947. Fulham Baths and Wash-houses were opened in 1902 and provided up-to-date facilities for the period. After reconstruction and modernization, they were officially reopened on 24 September 1937. Washing machines, hydro-extractors and drying horses were provided in addition to twelve hand-washing compartments. To complete the job, mangles and folding and ironing tables with electric irons were provided. This picture shows some of the hand-washing compartments and a hydro-extractor.

Employees of the Randell House Laundry, 51a Claxton Grove, at work in the ironing room, *c.* 1905. Along the centre of the table is a gas-fired contraption for heating the irons used by the laundry girls.

Fulham Borough Council's Maternity Home and Clinic, Parsons Green, *c*. 1950. Mothers with their children are collecting their allowances of National dried milk, concentrated orange juice and cod-liver oil. The maternity home, built by W.J. Marston & Son Ltd at a cost of about £40,000, opened on 16 October 1937 and replaced an earlier home at 706 Fulham Road.

Cleaning 'pig' bins at Munster Road Depot in the early 1950s. During the Second World War special communal bins for the collection of food waste, which was processed and sold to farmers, were placed around the borough. They were intensely disliked, as they were unpleasant and very smelly. The bins were finally removed early in 1954.

A posed photograph showing the Sampling Officer of the Medical Officer of Health's Department taking a milk sample in Cedarne Road, *c.* 1950. During 1950, 458 samples of milk were purchased for chemical analysis by the Public Analyst. Of these, 306 were purchased from milk vendors during the early delivery, 71 on Sundays and 72 during early morning deliveries to hospitals in the borough. It was found that water had been added to the milk in 1.02 per cent of the samples. All had been sold by the same vendor, who was fined £3 with costs on two occasions. No adulterations were reported the following year.

William Wingrave outside his greengrocer's shop at 415 North End Road, *c.* 1908. Among the goods on display are several types of potato, spring onions and spring flowers. William Wingrave served as a member of Fulham Vestry from 1888 to 1897.

An ambulance of the Fulham branch of the People's Dispensary for Sick Animals with a 'patient' in 1926. The branch opened at 2 Sandilands Road on 22 January 1925, after an experimental period when a caravan was allowed to stand in Effie Place for the treatment of the sick animals of the poor. In its first year the dispensary treated over 8,000 cases, including horses and donkeys.

The British Vacuum Cleaner Company, of Parsons Green Lane, at work at Waring & Gillow's furniture store, 168–182 Oxford Street. The vacuum cleaning process was invented in 1901 by Mr H. Cecil Booth, managing director of BVC, and world patents were acquired in 1903. In 1934 the *Fulham Chronicle* reported that: 'the BVC process has been used at Buckingham Palace and other royal palaces in Europe . . . the Houses of Parliament, the County Hall . . . public buildings and cinemas in Fulham, too, have been freed from dust and dirt . . . .'

The Olympia Garage at Addison Bridge Place, *c.* 1912. A full course of driving lessons could be had here for 5 guineas, with all-day tuition if it was required.

ENTERTAINMENT & LEISURE

Participants in the Battle of Naseby (1645), re-enacted at the Army Pageant in aid of The Incorporated Soldiers' and Sailors' Help Society, held at Fulham Palace in 1910. Mrs Christina Broom, photographer to The Household Brigade from 1904 to 1939, took this photograph.

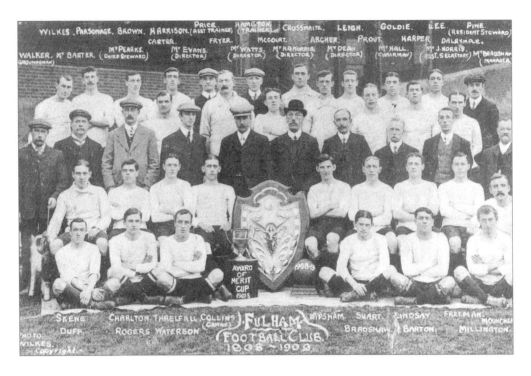

Fulham Football Club, originally Fulham St Andrews FC, was founded in 1879 and was closely linked to St Andrew's Church. The name was retained until 1888. The club used various grounds including Star Road, Eelbrook Common and Parsons Green before playing their first match at Craven Cottage in October 1896. The ground was built on the site of an old cottage, destroyed by fire in 1888. Ground levels were raised using soil from construction work on the Shepherds Bush to Bank tube line and road sweepings. The stand, fronting Stevenage Road, was designed by Archibald Leitch and opened in 1906. The top photograph shows the 1908/9 team, the bottom one shows fans arriving at the ground on a Cup-tie day, c. 1910.

The Hurlingham Club, well known for its many sporting activities, was founded in 1869 and still continues today. Pigeon shooting was the first sport on offer, later came polo, croquet, lawn tennis, swimming, ice-skating, ballooning, lacrosse, archery, golf, cricket and squash rackets. Polo was first played at Hurlingham in June 1874 and continued until 1939. Ballooning began during the summer of 1908 and lasted about six years. The club was able to make a small profit from supplying gas for the balloons. The top photograph shows King Alphonso of Spain playing for 'El Gordo' against 'Hurricanes' at Hurlingham in the 1920s and the lower photograph shows spectators watching the inflation of a balloon and the ascent of La Mascotte in 1908.

Captain F.A.M. Browning, DSO, (1896–1965) of the Grenadier Guards, competing in the Household Brigade Sports at Queen's Club in the 1920s. 'Boy' Browning was an Olympic athlete competing in the High Hurdles. Queen's Club was founded in 1886 and provided a home for various Oxford and Cambridge sporting events. Football, rugby and athletics plus a range of sports similar to those at Hurlingham were provided. Today the club is mainly known for rackets, real tennis and lawn tennis.

An evening class display involving fifteen gymnasts in the playground of Lillie Road School (now Sir John Lillie School), c. 1901. The evening classes, of which George Godley was Principal, began in the late 1890s.

Cowgirls in the Red Man Spectacle, part of the Golden West and American (USA) Industries Exhibition, Earls Court, 1909. Visitors could enjoy the spectacle in the Empress Theatre, which depicted Sioux Indians going into camp for the night and in the morning performing dances to the rising sun and other Red Indian gods. A display of steer roping and bronco busting by cowgirls and cowboys followed and finally a re-enactment of the Black Hawk Massacre took place. Reserved seats for the spectacle cost 1s, 2s and 3s and included admission to the Red Indian Camp.

The men's second-class swimming pool at Fulham Baths after the modernization and reconstruction scheme of 1936/7. The Baths and Wash-houses, designed by Mr Dighton Pearson and costing £74,000, were officially opened on 10 April 1902. The Mayor, Councillor W.R. Sayer, took the first plunge after replacing his frock coat with a scantier but more suitable costume. There were two pools for men and one for ladies, plus the laundry and private baths.

The Cambridge boat and crew which competed in the Oxford and Cambridge Universities Boat Race on 1 April 1911. Oxford won by 2¾ lengths in 18 minutes 29 seconds. This is another photograph by the local photographer Mrs Christina Broom (1863–1939).

Visitors to the Western Gardens, seen here during the Balkan States Exhibition at Earls Court in 1907, would have been able to listen to military bands, visit a salt mine or take a ride on the switchback railway. Other amusements at the exhibition included the Balkan stalactite caverns, a gondola ride, the Balkan Theatre and Sir Hiram Maxim's captive airship.

The dismantling of the great wheel at Earls Court in 1907. The wheel was built to the plans of Mr W.B. Basset and began to turn on 5 July 1895. It was 284 feet in diameter, constructed of mild steel and made an average of thirty journeys a day. During its life it travelled about 9,350 miles through the air.

The grand finale of the Army Pageant, Fulham Palace, 20 June–2 July 1910. Two temporary bridges over the moat gave access to the stands which had been used in the English Church Pageant the previous year. Large numbers of regular troops were involved, supplemented by local residents. A choir of 300 was accompanied by a band of 200 musicians and local school children were able to attend two dress rehearsals.

Bull terriers owned by E.T. Pimm, licensee of The Cock hotel, 360 North End Road, with their handler (whose identity is unknown) on Eelbrook Common, *c.* 1908. Mr Pimm was well known for his sporting interests. From left to right are: 'East Hill Daisy', Champion 'Sam Lavender', 'Bob Lavington' and 'St James Beauty'.

The Red Hall Cinema, 1914. The 1,600 seater cinema in Vanston Place, designed by Mr H. George Leslie, was opened on 18 December 1913. A screening of *David Copperfield* followed the ceremony. It was renamed the Gaumont Cinema in 1950 and the Walham Green Gaumont in 1956 and closed on 8 December 1962, reopening a few days later as a bingo hall.

The Grand Theatre, *c.* 1903. Situated at the foot of Putney Bridge, the theatre was built in white Portland stone to the designs of Mr W.G.R. Sprague. When it opened on 23 August 1897 it seated 2,239 people. Mixed fortunes resulted in closures and name changes, and it was also used as a cinema. The theatre was demolished in 1957/8 and replaced by offices.

The Wheatsheaf public house, 580 Fulham Road (now The Sporting Rat). This brick building, opened in May 1890, replaced an earlier pub demolished in 1889. The new pub was designed by Messrs Fletcher and Hynam and built by Mr Gerrard. The *Fulham Chronicle* described it as a 'handsome and commodious house'. A billiard room, lavatories and stabling were provided for the convenience of its customers.

The Swan Inn, a picturesque property with tea gardens running down to the river, photographed some time before its destruction by fire on 18 September 1871. The inn was said to have been built in 1698. To the right of the inn can be seen the tower of nearby All Saints Church.

Old-time dancing at Fulham Town Hall in the early 1950s. An Old Time Dance Club was formed in 1951 with admission charges of 1s to members and 1s 6d to non-members. The club met on Monday nights and membership rose from 71 people in October 1951 to 164 in March 1952. As dancing was so popular, the council decided to introduce an Old Time Dance session on the fourth Monday in each month in place of the club session. Demand for these was so great that the council were persuaded to introduce another dance on one Saturday a month, beginning in May 1952.

Storytime for younger children at Fulham Junior Library, *c.* 1936. The storyteller is probably Miss Doris Chilcot who was appointed Children's Librarian in June 1936. Visits were made to the three libraries in the borough by 512 classes during 1936 and Miss Chilcot made thirty-seven visits to schools to talk to teachers and children.

A chess tournament organized by Fulham Junior Library, in the lecture hall of Fulham Central Library during the 1930s. Extension activities were considered very important as a means of introducing children to the world of books. Films, lectures, exhibitions, a stamp club, competitions and even puppet shows were available to those who were interested.

A carnival float from a procession in aid of the War Memorial Fund and Fulham District Nursing Association, *c.* 1920. Plans to raise £20,000 to build a War Memorial and a Fulham District Nursing Institution from private donations, dances and other entertainments failed. Instead the money was devoted to the Fulham District Nursing Association, which had been founded in 1920.

24th Fulham (Sands End) Scout troop with their float 'Royal Barge', which took part in the Coronation Scout Week procession on 27 June 1953. The procession, which was nearly a mile long, included decorated lorries, hand carts, bicycles and wheel barrows. Over 500 Scouts and Cubs and dozens of other local organizations participated. The Scout troop's float was described as 'outstanding'.

An unusual photograph of British Boy Scouts, whose meetings were held in Townmead Road School, parading in Bagleys Lane. The British Boys Scouts broke away from the Boy Scouts in 1909 when their founder Sir Frances Vain, a London Commissioner, thought that the Scout movement was becoming too militaristic.

One of the murals in the Haig Memorial Hall, Royal British Legion Club, New Kings Road, painted by Glyn Jones in 1950. The work took ten weeks and cost £186 for 130 square yards, plus £23 for a protective coating of beeswax. The scene depicts an idealized view of Samuel Richardson's house at Parsons Green, which stood approximately on the site of the club, and the surrounding area. At present the murals are boarded over to protect them from damage.

Fulham Vestrymen and Officers at their annual Beanfeast at Rye House, Hoddesdon, 24 July 1897. About 360 employees caught the 9.05 a.m. train from Chelsea Station for a day in the country. On arrival, the *Fulham Chronicle* commented: 'It was soon evident that the Fulham Vestry employees had been there before, and the locations of the various refreshment houses were impressed upon their minds with a geographical accuracy that would do credit to an explorer of the Arctic regions.' Dinner and tea were served and, in between, a cricket match was played and fishing and athletics races took place. They returned home at about 9.30 p.m. Cemetery workers, unable to attend, were given a day's leave and extra pay.

INDEX

BRITAIN IN OLD PHOTOGRAPHS

To order any of these titles please telephone our distributor, Littlehampton Book Services on 01903 721596
For a catalogue of these and our other titles please ring Regina Schinner on 01453 731114